The photographs on page 9 are reproduced by permission of the Trustees of the British Museum (Natural History).

Published by A & C Black (Publishers) Ltd
35 Bedford Row, London WC1R 4JH

First published 1978
© 1978 Pat and Helen Clay
Reprinted 1983

ISBN 0-7136-1813-2

Printed in Hong Kong by Dai Nippon Printing Co. Ltd

NATURE IN CLOSE-UP

THE DRAGONFLY

PAT AND HELEN CLAY

ADAM & CHARLES BLACK · LONDON

Contents

What are dragonflies?

Dragonflies are dramatically coloured insects. They spend most of their lives as nymphs at the bottom of ponds, rivers and streams until they are ready to emerge and fly.

Most dragonflies are fast flyers. In warm sunny weather they swoop and dart over the water. They fly at speeds up to 100 kilometres an hour. You would be lucky to get close to a dragonfly resting on a bush like the one on the opposite page.

Like most insects, dragonflies have compound eyes. This means that their eyes have up to 30 000 facets, each with its own little view. They help the dragonfly to find food and spot enemies.

Dragonflies are carnivorous (meat-eating). They feed mainly on flies, mosquitoes, gnats and bees. They don't harm people. Nor do they attack cattle, though some people think they do. A dragonfly is only after the swarm of flies which buzzes round the cow's head. The family name for dragonflies, *Odonata*, means 'toothed creature'.

Dragonfly restin
on a ree

Dragonflies of the past

Fossil dragonflies have been found which date back 300 million years. They lived in what is known as the Carboniferous age.

This was a time when huge forests covered the earth. Ferns, mare's tails and mosses grew to heights of up to 20 metres. Huge dragonflies with wing-spans of up to 60 centimetres flew among these tree-like plants. The remains of the world's oldest dragonfly have recently been discovered 915 metres below ground at Bolsover Colliery, Derbyshire, England.

On the opposite page are some later dragonfly fossils. They come from the Jurassic period, 150 million years ago. By this time dragonflies were smaller and more like the ones we know today.

Complete
fossilized
dragonfly

Incomplete
fossilized
dragonfly

Mating

On warm summer days, male dragonflies chase females over water or among riverside reeds. Eventually the male swoops down on a female. He grasps her by the neck with a pair of claspers at the end of his body. The female curves her body up towards his and mating takes place as shown in the picture below.

Sometimes the pair will fly together, the male towing the female 'in tandem'. Some male dragonflies continue to support the female by the neck while she is laying eggs. This is a dangerous time, when frogs and newts may attack her. She may also get her wings water-logged and drown.

Egg laying

Nymphs, as the young dragonflies are called, hatch from the eggs the female has laid. In this picture (right) you can see dragonfly eggs and some newly-hatched nymphs.

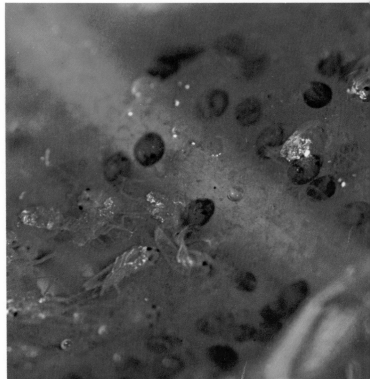

Dragonfly nymphs

The nymphs live from one to five years in the
mud at the bottom of ponds, streams and rivers.
Like the full-grown dragonfly, the nymph is
carnivorous. With its lower lip, sometimes
called a mask or shovel, the nymph scoops up
any passing small fish, tadpole or worm.

Dragonfly nymph

As the nymph grows, it sheds its outer skin many times. Eventually it is ready to make the final change into an adult dragonfly. This is a dangerous time for the nymph as it is easily attacked by ducks and other birds. In the right-hand picture (bottom) you can see a crab spider attacking an unwary damselfly (a type of dragonfly. See page 20).

Preparing to Emerge

During its life under water the nymph grows bigger and its body changes in several ways. When the insect is about half-grown the shape of its wing-cases can be seen clearly. The nymph becomes more active.

It crawls around the bottom of the pond and sometimes 'swims' near the surface. Soon it develops so that it can breathe either underwater or in air.

The nymph can now be much more adventurous. It often leaves the pond or stream for short walks. It is almost ready to become a dragonfly. The nymph in the photograph below is leaving the pond for good.

When it has left the pond, the nymph will seek a suitable firm stalk or reed and begin to climb to the top.

When the nymph has anchored its legs to the support, it rests for a while. It is waiting to become a dragonfly.

Emergence

1. The changing or emergence of a dragonfly often takes place early in the day. First the outer skin of the nymph splits near the neck. The split widens and the head of a dragonfly begins to appear.

2. The insect pulls itself out of the skin quite quickly. Soon all the legs are free and only the tail-end, the abdomen of the dragonfly, is left clinging to the inside of the case.

3. By this time the dragonfly is hanging head downwards. It rests for a while as it prepares for the next most critical stage of the emergence, the 'flip-up'.

4. The 'flip-up' is done by a sudden, upward, swinging movement of the body as the insect finally drags itself completely free. If the dragonfly can't get a firm grip in this position, it will fall to the ground, damage its wings, and be unable to fly.

The final stage of this transformation is the 'drying out'. While the dragonfly rests after its efforts, it pumps air and fluid into its veins.

The wings lose their milky appearance and become transparent. Suddenly they lower and fix permanently into an outstretched position. After a few experimental flutterings, the adult dragonfly soars away on its first flight.

The hole fr[om]
which the dragon[fly]
has emerg[ed]

The nymphal case

On a day when many dragonflies have emerged, dozens of empty cases, like the one on the left, can be found draped on bushes.

The top right-hand picture (opposite) shows the hole from which the dragonfly has safely emerged. The white threads inside are the tubes through which the nymph breathed.

The bottom right-hand picture (opposite) shows the hinged mask of the nymph's lower lip. When it is not in use, it is tucked away, masking part of the face. The lip shoots out when the hungry nymph spots a passing prey. Sharp pincers at the end of the lip keep hold of the nymph's meal.

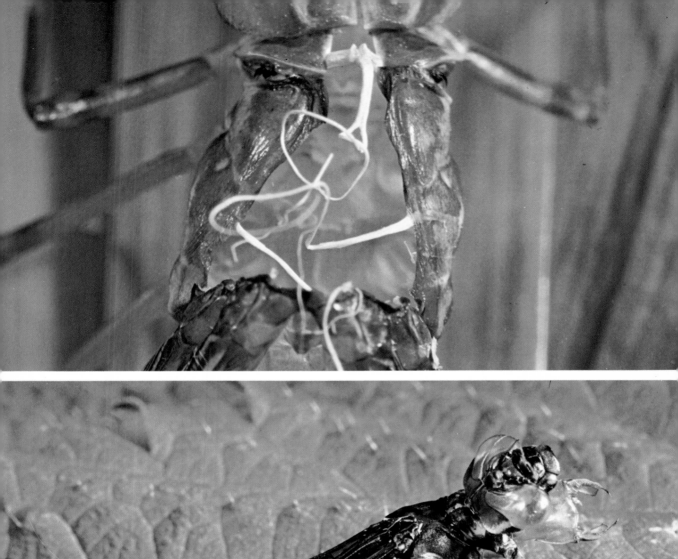

Different types of dragonfly

There are many different types of dragonfly. The four groups you are most likely to find are Hawkers, Darters, Agrions and Damselflies.

Hawkers
Named for their fast 'hawk-like' style of flight, these dragonflies are large and brightly-coloured.

The males always fight fiercely to defend their own stretch of water from intruders. Among the Hawkers we find the Aeshna dragonflies (see below), the lovely Golden-ringed and the dramatic blue and black Emperor. The full-grown Hawker has a wing-span of up to ten centimetres and a body length of seven centimetres.

Common sympetrum (male)

Darters
These are slightly smaller than Hawkers, but they are just as colourful. They make short darting flights before returning to a familiar perch. Among the Darters are the Sympetrums (see photographs), the Four-spotted and Broad-bodied Libellulas and the green Downy Emerald.

Common Sympetrum — immature

Common Sympetrum — mature

Agrions

The Agrion is smaller and less powerful than the true dragonfly. Unlike Hawkers and Darters, who rest with wings outstretched, the male *Agrion virgo* (above left) is either brilliant blue or green and his wings shimmer in the sunlight. The female (above right) is a sandy brown colour. You will recognise the *Agrion splendens* or Banded Agrion which has a cloudy patch of darker colour on its wings.

Damselflies

These are the smallest members of the dragonfly family. They too are very colourful and rest with their wings closed. On a sunny day you can see bright blue Common Ischnuras, Green Lestes, Large Red and Variable Coenagrion.

Colour change

Newly-emerged dragonflies
are usually a pale
yellowish-green colour.
They stay like this for several
days. They then mature into
their brighter mixture of
reds, greens, blues and
yellows.

Dragonfly just
before its
first flight

The life of a dragonfly is
short. Some species only live
a few weeks. As the insect
ages, its colour changes once
again. Parts of the body
become covered by a pale
blue powder. After death the
dragonfly's colours fade very
quickly.

Dragonfly in
old age

If you want to look for dragonflies, the most useful thing to carry is a pocket magnifying glass. Approach the dragonfly with care as it can see any sudden movement up to 12 metres away.

The dragonfly has a large head connected to a very slender neck. The head balances the body and makes flying easy. The front pair of wings work separately from the back pair and make it possible for the dragonfly to fly in any direction, even backwards. It can hover like a helicopter (below) as well.

The dragonfly's head and eyes

Where dragonflies live

Dragonflies like almost any patch of water, but some species prefer particular types of water.

The Common Aeshna likes the acid water that is found on heath and moorland.

The Four-spotted Libellula prefers stagnant ponds.

Lakes and pools, like the one below, are the favourite haunt of the Emperor dragonfly.

Agrions like to fly along streams like the one opposite and other dragonflies are found over gravel pits, bogs or marshland.

Sometimes dragonflies fly away from water altogether. They can then be found perched on top of hedges or resting in a sunny woodland glade. You may even see them in towns.

Many dragonflies migrate to other countries where great swarms of them have been reported flying over big cities.

Wherever we live we can almost always find dragonflies, but we have to go out and look for them.